Checklist
for Leaders

Management Master Series

William F. Christopher
Editor in Chief

Set 4: Leadership

Burt Nanus
Leading the Way to Organization Renewal

Gabriel Hevesi
Checklist for Leaders

Karl Albrecht
Creating Leaders for Tomorrow

D. Otis Wolkins
Total Quality: A Framework for Leadership

Lawrence M. Miller
From Management to Leadership

Leonard R. Sayles
*High Performance Leadership:
Creating Value in a World of Change*

Checklist
for Leaders

Gabriel Hevesi

PRODUCTIVITY PRESS
Portland, Oregon

Management Master Series
William F. Christopher, Editor in Chief

Productivity Press
P.O. Box 13390
Portland, OR 97213-0390
United States of America
Telephone: 503-235-0600
Telefax: 503-235-0909
E-mail: service@ppress.com

Book design by William Stanton
Cover illustration by Paul Zwolak
Page design, graphics, and composition by Rohani Design, Edmonds, Washington
Printed and bound by BookCrafters in the United States of America

Library of Congress Cataloging-in-Publication Data

Hevesi, Gabriel.
    Checklist for leaders / Gabriel Hevesi
       p.   cm. — (Management master series. Set 4, Leadership)
    Includes bibliographic references (pp. 75, 76).
    ISBN 1-56327-152-4. — ISBN 1-56327-100-1 (pbk.)
    1. Leadership. 2. Decision making. I. Title. II. Series.
    HD57. 7.H48   1995
    658.4' 92—dc20
                                                    95-44171
                                                        CIP

02 01 00 99 98 97 96 10 9 8 7 6 5 4 3 2

— CONTENTS —

PUBLISHER'S MESSAGE

The *Management Master Series* was designed to discover and disseminate to you the world's best concepts, principles, and current practices in excellent management. We present this information in a concise and easy-to-use format to provide you with the tools and techniques you need to stay abreast of this rapidly accelerating world of ideas.

World class competitiveness requires managers today to be thoroughly informed about how and what other internationally successful managers are doing. What works? What doesn't? and Why?

Management is often considered a "neglected art." It is not possible to know how to manage before you are made a manager. But once you become a manager you are expected to know how to manage and to do it well, right from the start.

One result of this neglect in management training has been managers who rely on control rather than creativity. Certainly, managers in this century have shown a distinct neglect of workers as creative human beings. The idea that employees are an organization's most valuable asset is still very new. How managers can inspire and direct the creativity and intelligence of everyone involved in the work of an organization has only begun to emerge.

Perhaps if we consider management as a "science" the task of learning how to manage well will be easier. A scientist begins with an hypothesis and then runs experiments to observe whether the hypothesis is correct. Scientists depend on detailed notes about the experiment—the timing, the ingredients, the amounts—and carefully record all results as they test new hypotheses. Certain things come to be known by this method; for instance, that water always consists of one part oxygen and two parts hydrogen.

We as managers must learn from our experience and from the experience of others. The scientific approach provides a model for learning. Science begins with vision and desired outcomes, and achieves its purpose through observation, experiment, and analysis of precisely recorded results. And then what is newly discovered is shared so that each person's research will build on the work of others.

Our organizations, however, rarely provide the time for learning or experimentation. As a manager, you need information from those who have already experimented and learned and recorded their results. You need it in brief, clear, and detailed form so that you can apply it immediately.

It is our purpose to help you confront the difficult task of managing in these turbulent times. As the shape of leadership changes, the *Management Master Series* will continue to bring you the best learning available to support your own increasing artistry in the evolving science of management.

We at Productivity Press are grateful to William F. Christopher and our staff of editors who have searched out those masters with the knowledge, experience, and ability to write concisely and completely on excellence in management practice. We wish also to thank the individual volume authors; Diane Asay, project manager; Julie Zinkus, manuscript editor; Karen Jones, managing editor; Lisa Hoberg and Mary Junewick, editorial support; Bill Stanton, design and production management; Susan Swanson, production coordination; Rohani Design, graphics, page design, and composition.

Norman Bodek
Publisher

INTRODUCTION

Good advice, whomever it comes from, depends on the shrewdness of the prince who seeks it.

—N. Machiavelli

There is no recipe for success. If there were, we all would use it and it would cease to be effective. Yet many roads can lead to success. The secret is to choose the right road for your organization among all options. It takes skilled judgment to apply the right method, at the right time, under the right circumstances. Using sound judgment, we know when to act, when to coach, and when to delegate.

Checklist for Leaders provides checkpoints for day-by-day decisions and actions. It covers the essence of:

- leadership
- communication
- team-building
- planning
- efficiency
- decision making

The emphasis is on usefulness. The book presents often opposing theories and opinions to provoke, to force thinking—to fit variables together like pieces in a jigsaw puzzle.

Visualize, compare, and project your own situation while reading, and select any ideas and methods that are useful to you.

A true test of leadership is how you use your judgment and common sense for selection, timing, and application of ideas.

The *Checklist* does not include case studies of success or failure in large organizations. Presumably you are not the president of G.E., nor involved in the particular situation of, say, IBM or GM. Your problems are different. Their case is not yours. Since every case is unique, case studies become mere anecdotes. They are good reading, but do little to help you solve your problems.

The *Checklist* aims to be practical, to help you with ideas to build your own success story.

1

COMMON SENSE
AND SOUND JUDGMENT

MANAGEMENT IDEAS

Management ideas evolve as conditions change—as the need to change arises. Winning ideas match reality best. Victor Hugo remarked: "Greater than the tread of mighty armies is an idea whose time has come."

There are no ready-to-wear solutions. And beware: Even the best ideas succeed only if you use common sense to apply them. As W. Edwards Deming sums it up: "One of the obstacles of quality transformation is searching for a ready-made quality recipe, instead of creating one that meets the organization's unique requirements."[1] Each case is special—each situation unique. Only the broadest guidelines and common sense fit every case and situation.

Without the use of common sense and sound judgment, other important management skills are wasted and processes fail. A *leader* applies common sense and avoids extremes. He or she directs, rather than dominates; is involved, but not lost in details; delegates without trying to avoid ultimate responsibility. A leader uses judgment when under pressure from above to be iron-handed, and pressure from below to delegate all.

The cost of failing to use judgment and common sense can be high. More promising careers end due to bad judgment than to failing to apply one method or another.

Reasoning must precede choosing a path to follow or taking action. Sir William Drumond painted the picture for us: "He who will not reason is a bigot; he who cannot, is a fool; and he who does not, is a slave."

Visualize management ideas as highways—as roads to success. Most run parallel, some intersect. Others widen to accommodate different users. Some transform into new highways. Many open new territories. Some start from old secondary roads. A few originate as new turnpikes. Some are "in," others "out." Drivers who exceed speed limits and cut curves to get somewhere faster may end up paying for failure. The experienced driver knows each curve, each danger zone, and at what speed to travel. Hotheads collide and run off the road. Those who do not study the map may head in the wrong direction. Does it sound familiar? Does it look familiar?

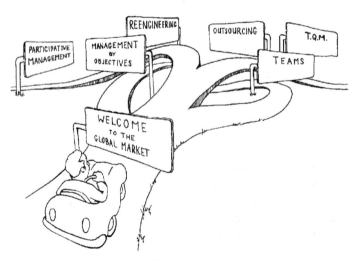

Figure 1. Which Road to Follow?

CHOOSING MANAGEMENT IDEAS

Most management ideas evolve from "old secondary roads" that only a few people used. As more people became aware of them, as conditions changed, they were widened, conceptualized, modernized to meet new requirements. The old road, paved and improved, became a highway now shown on every map and available to all.

Selecting a highway depends on where you want to go and how to get there; on your determination, resistance to fatigue, your resources; your goals and priorities; your travel companions. You can also combine stretches of different roads that serve you best.

Always use judgment. As a leader, you must take practical approaches to theories and systems:

- Choose what fits your requirements, not what is popular.
- Use resources—institutional, human, material— to best advantage.
- Apply complementary concepts and avoid mutually exclusive ones.
- Be effective, not dogmatic.
- Be master, not slave, of ideas and methods.

Winning companies have a risk-taking, entrepreneurial culture; they reflect the leader.

Beware of pitfalls. The most common are:

- *Being so involved in day-to-day details and crisis management that you have no time for creative ideas.* Set time aside—an hour a day, one day a week, whatever suits you—to sit back and think. It's your most productive time.

- *Forgetting important goals and priorities when you're dealing with immediate problems.* It's easy to be carried away with short-term success and forget the main objective. For example, persuading a client to accept defective merchandise can mean "win now, lose later." Always keep a mental blackboard in front of you, with the principal objective(s) written in large letters.

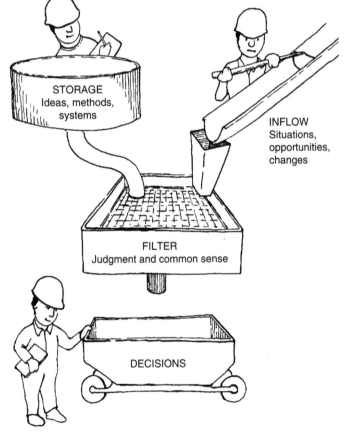

Figure 2. Leaders Filter Ideas, Evaluate Situations, Seize Opportunities—Always Using Sound Judgment.

Win the war, not the battle. A satisfied client is worth far more than a quick sale.

A good idea is like a newly designed car: smart, futuristic, a challenge to what exists. Yet, as nice as this car might be to look at, without practical application—without a driver, roads, and fuel—it is useless. A good idea also needs a driver (leader), roads (opportunity), and fuel (moving force).

CHECKLIST

- Use sound judgment and choose the right priorities. Success depends on them.

- Never underestimate common sense.

- Each business situation requires its own solution. Create the one that matches and supports your organization's vision, goals, character, and values.

2

MANAGERS LEAD

The world challenges managers to lead: to create new strategies and positioning; to make wise decisions, guided by keen awareness of the world around us. In today's business environment leaders must face the following issues and challenges:

- Relationships inside the organization and outside—with peers, clients, and suppliers; the authorities and the public; environmentalists and the media; all of these, both local and foreign. All demand special knowledge, talent, and dedication.

- Problems and opportunities that arise from social and economic change, from new technologies, from rapidly changing market trends, and from variations in foreign exchange rates, taxes, and duties.

- Innovation throughout the organization, improved multidirectional communication, strategic thinking, and creative action—all are essential for success and even for survival.

- Quality, service, and price that satisfy rapidly increasing consumer expectations. Business ethics and work ethics are getting deserved visibility.

MEETING THE CHALLENGES

To meet these challenges, managers must become agents of change in attitude and actions. However, they must not convert their units into experimental labs for new concepts. At the same time, utterances such as "We tried this before and it did not work," or "We always used this form/system/technique successfully, why change?" must not be heard again.

- Leader-managers think and evaluate options.
- They involve their peers and reports in setting goals.
- They make it happen.

The leader's attitude is fundamental. Whether it is results-oriented or not, it reflects throughout the organization—the higher the position, the greater the influence. The importance the boss gives to quality, client satisfaction, the environment, and the treatment of employees is contagious and impacts the future of the enterprise.

Creativity is an example. The organization that is quick to punish mistakes and slow to recognize new ideas destroys the enthusiasm of creative people and eventually loses them.

CONVENTIONAL METHODS
ARE OUTMODED NOW

Ideas and goals must replace habits in an environment of continuous innovation and entrepreneurial spirit. Organizations must be outward-looking and future-oriented, not inward-looking or past-oriented. Customer satisfaction must become the number-one priority. No more trying to get away with the minimum, if complaints are not too loud. Companies must satisfy internal clients as well as external clients. Team spirit to work toward common goals must replace interdepartmental rivalries.

Moving ahead (forward-looking)

Looks ahead through the windshield:

- New strategies
- New positioning
- New goals (dynamic)

Rolling back (inward-looking)

Looks backward through the mirror:

- Past experience
- Past success
- Why change? (static)

CHECKLIST

- Lead the change, whatever your present level. Don't risk being left behind. (How many innovations did you make happen lately?)

- Don't simply manage people—lead them.

- Spell out your ideas loud and clear. No one hears a mute.

Leaders are needed everywhere: the shopfloor, the lab, the office, in work teams or sales.

3

WHAT MAKES A LEADER?

Leadership is not limited to the chairman. Leaders exist at all levels of the organization. Not all managers are leaders, however—only the good ones are. And not all leaders are managers.

Leaders are made, not born. Leadership is a mix of skills, attitude, will, and motivation. To become a leader, you must want it, work on it. It requires much effort to get there and remain there.

Managing, on the other hand, is an assignment—a job. A manager who is not a leader manages by title only. A leader-manager inspires people, sets an example, and builds trust. He or she:

- makes things happen

- is mentor and coach

- is respected and followed

- has a clear purpose

- single-mindedly pursues common goals, regardless of obstacles or temporary setbacks

- leads people to accomplish what they thought impossible, freeing them from their inhibitions and limitations

Leaders don't compromise. They want the best. If they are satisfied with mediocre results, that is what they achieve. A good manager is a leader through personality, not position.

True leaders impact their organization. They are strong. They attract people and receive support from peers and employees. They draw followers by their ability to communicate vision and commitment. They make their ideas tangible and create positive feelings. They are reliable and effective. Two comments by a great leader, Sir Winston Churchill, come to mind:

> *Those who are not prepared to take unpopular decisions and to face up to challenges are not worthy of being Ministers of State in time of stress.*

> *I cannot give you a form for success. But I can give you a sure-fire formula for failure: just try to please everyone.*

A LEADER IS A CHANGE LEADER

A leader overcomes resistance to change from those who fear losing security, power, or status; and those who fear change because of limited skill, knowledge, or experience. A leader

- educates
- motivates
- communicates
- supports
- leads change
- turns every situation into a learning experience

A LEADER IS A COACH

A leader wants others to improve and guides, rather than controls, them. A leader is proud of the success of others, not jealous. He or she trusts people. Trust creates trust and loyalty. Who cannot be trusted must leave. A leader

- builds positive relationships
- is frank and critical, but not threatening
- is a keen observer
- knows how to ask questions and evaluate answers

A leader develops people's potential, instead of judging their performance.

A LEADER MOTIVATES

He or she sets the strongest motivators in motion:

- *Belonging:* being a member of the team
- *Achieving:* reaching common goals—the more difficult, the greater the satisfaction
- *Recognition:* praise, promotion, rewards

William N. Yoeman[2] ranks the creation of a motivating environment among the most important functions of the leader. Motivation toward common goals strengthens emotional ties among members of a team and with their leader.

A LEADER COMMUNICATES AND LEADS CHANGE

A leader gives support, discusses goals, and influences by inspiration, not by imposition.

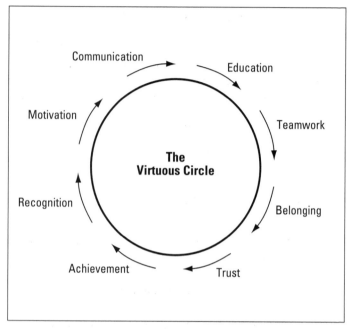

Figure 3. The Virtuous Circle

He or she

- is not embarrassed to ask for advice

- eliminates the we/they barrier between line and staff, production and sales, or competing locations

- is self-confident and does not need a "common enemy" to achieve unity

- encourages creativity and innovation and is receptive to new ideas

- accepts mistakes, if not repeated, as opportunities to learn

- gets things done with or without direct authority

As a *boss,* a leader

- is an ally, not a competitor
- is generous with praise for a job well done
- makes his or her expectations clear
- is specific in criticism and gives honest feedback
- maintains personal and functional (rather than hierarchical) relationships
- welcomes differing points of view to help in finding best solutions
- leads to reach common goals
- chooses the right people for the right job

A LEADER'S QUALITIES

To list all the qualities of a leader is an impossible task. Not only is the list long, but many of the qualities may seem to be mutually exclusive. A leader can be

- dynamic and/or patient
- forceful and/or sensitive
- creative and/or down to earth
- decisive and/or restrictive

In short, a leader combines creative dynamism with practicality.

THE EMERGING PROFILE OF A LEADER

He or she

- is authentic—sets examples and priorities
- is committed—coaches, motivates, communicates

- challenges conventional wisdom
- leads change and innovation
- trusts, and builds trust
- is courageous—knows right from wrong and does what's right, regardless of the consequences
- is results-oriented—fights resolutely for an idea
- is demanding, but fair—uses authority, but is not authoritarian
- is entrepreneurial
- is a team-builder—members have complementary skills
- sets trends—he or she is followed, not a follower
- is energetic

Alexander Hamilton, one of the fathers of the American Constitution said, "Energy in the Executive is a leading character of good government,"—and of business enterprise.

THE PROFILE OF A DEMAGOGUE

What about sham leaders—dictators, or that person you know? He or she

- is usually charismatic
- is suspicious, building dependence, not trust
- feels threatened by the success of others
- is surrounded by "yes-men"
- submits to superiors, is harsh on subordinates
- is authoritarian, managing by intimidation

- plays to the public, saying what they want to hear

- creates an object of hate—a "common enemy"

- fights for personal interest, blaming others

- feels insecure and fearful

- gets results at any price

Such people think they are leaders. In fact, they are the opposite—nuisances at best, or even public enemies.

CHECKLIST

- Go back to the list in "The Emerging Profile of a Leader" and check off the qualities you possess.

- Of those you don't, select three you are keen to possess. Establish a time limit, say, twelve months. Start developing those qualities now.

- Rate your peers by the same measure. Assist them in improving. Everyone will benefit.

Leadership is the result of strong willpower, hard work, vision, and choosing the right priorities.

4

LEADERS COMMUNICATE

Multimedia is at our doorstep. TV, cable, and magazines fight for attention. Media messages inundate our homes—by mail, phone, newsletters. Newspapers have gone electronic. Creative people are highly paid to get marketing messages across to the public. But good internal communication is sadly lacking in many companies.

If risk-taking is the essence of business, communication is its nerve center. It was important even in the "old days" when the business climate was steadier—rules were known; procedures were standard; organization charts rigid; and so were job descriptions. Everyone had clearly defined roles and responsibilities.

COMMUNICATING TODAY

Times have changed, and so have organizations. Rules have become more flexible. New situations and challenges arise daily in this turbulent business climate. Fast reaction is a *must*, yet not possible without good communication. Everyone needs information to work as a team striving to achieve common goals and to share responsibilities.

A computer breakdown can be a serious problem. It causes interruptions, delays, and extra cost. Yet, we often ignore the more costly breakdown of internal communication. Incomplete information or a lack of information seriously affects our involvement, our sharing of goals, and our teamwork.

A breakdown in communication results in

- rumor mills due to unreliable information
- wrong information due to interpretation, distraction, and incomplete information
- conflicting priorities among peers or departments

As a leader, your signals for direction must be clear and easy to follow. If the brake lights of your car don't work, or you don't use your blinkers when turning, you may cause a bad accident.

Leading without the necessary information is like dispatching a mission without a briefing. An unknown target cannot be met. Managing without information is like target-shooting blindfolded. Working without information is an activity with no results, or wrong results.

Consider what can happen when we don't communicate:

- A promotional campaign is launched and delivery committed by sales. The cash forecast is based on these sales. Meanwhile, purchasing was not advised to order raw materials and there are none at the plant.

- A reporting deadline was anticipated and several departments are on overtime to comply. Meanwhile, the accountant is on leave and the mainframe is being overhauled.

- Management announces a major change in product mix, requiring a different distribution. Meanwhile, sales commissions were just modified and a long-term supply contract signed, all based on the old mix.

Does it sound familiar?

These examples refer to the flow of basic information and coordination. But real communication is more.

Real Communication

Real communication opens the tap for unrestricted flow of information. It's not an easy process. It must be gradual. It requires trust and courage. To maintain credibility, management must strictly follow its own message. Real communication is based on mutual trust.

In this process, we must treat all people equally and encourage ideas, whoever they come from. Evaluation and feedback are essential, even on ideas that don't seem practical for implementation.

There must be an open exchange of ideas among peers and between managers and their reports. No shying away from delicate subjects to avoid friction. Insist on openness all around. Information must reach all levels and involve everyone to reach common goals.

In summary, everyone must

- become familiar with the organization's philosophy

- be informed on goals and plans

- become part of the action—involved and motivated

- communicate freely

There should be no fear of giving away secrets (secrets seldom are secrets) or suffering negative consequences.

Among all forms of communication, nothing equals a face-to-face exchange. There is no substitute for body language. The tone, facial expressions, and gestures that go with the words cannot be expressed in writing or even over the phone.

Ten Tips for Improving Communication

1. **Manage by walking around. Interact with as many people as possible, at all levels.** Walk around. Comment on company business, problems, opportunities, and plans. Communicate informally.

2. **Substitute one-on-one exchange for unproductive meetings.** Learn by listening. Make your message clear. Achieve more in less time.

3. **Reduce layers and stretch the organization horizontally.** Communication will be faster, more reliable.

4. **Make the organization flexible.** Avoid rigid organization charts and restrictive job descriptions. Flexibility allows new situations to be met fast by rearranging the troops, by forming ad-hoc teams. Informality lifts barriers in communication.

5. **Make written communication short and clear.** To the point. Easy to understand. Avoid excessive explanations and arguments.

6. **Learn to listen.** It provides information to the president or the sales person. The talkative sales person cannot hear the customer. A good listener does not interrupt, but shows interest and tries to understand the other party—what makes him or her tick.

7. **Accept frank opinions from peers and employees.** Criticism is communication too. Don't shoot the messenger.

8. **Think before you communicate.** Consider the other party; anticipate reactions. Don't tell people only what they want to hear. Give bad news in a sensitive way.

9. **Stay well informed.** Via networking; interacting with colleagues, clients, and suppliers; with others connected to the business. Their input is important.

10. **Other methods.** Include information to new hires; periodical briefings; information on notice boards; a professionally edited newsletter, using appropriate language to boost team spirit and promote new ideas.

Listening

Among all points listed, the one that deserves special emphasis is listening. Everyone needs to develop the ability to use more and more available (and often unused) listening capacity. Learn to concentrate on what's being said. Avoid distractions. Grasp the essential and withhold anticipated judgment.

As Tom Peters[3] points out, listening is fundamental to sharing information and goals; to getting involvement and mutual understanding; to achieving team targets.

Listening enriches with knowledge and gives recognition to the other person. As a John Updike character observes: "...that's what we all want from each other: recognition."[4]

CHECKLIST

- Communication is recognition. Even a reprimand is preferred to being ignored.

- If you want people to listen to you, learn to listen to them.

- Do you listen with care? Communicate more than what's essential? Do you pay and receive attention when you talk to your peers, superiors, or reports?

Communication is an irrigation of ideas. Without it everything dries.

COMMUNICATING, OBSERVING, NEGOTIATING

No one is the same as anyone else. A good communicator/negotiator is a keen observer of behavior. Observation discloses valuable information and helps effective communication.

Behavior patterns emerge from the way people talk, walk, and shake hands, from the decoration of an office, and the attitude of a secretary. These clues are important, not only to sales people, but to everyone who communicates or negotiates.

As a parallel, think of market research: researchers observe, then quantify behavior: people's needs and desires, their likes and dislikes. From this they formulate an advertising message that penetrates—and package goods that please.

Behavior Patterns

Some of the most typical behavior patterns, and how to respond to them, are listed below:

- *High flier:* Efficient, action-oriented, fast, impatient.
  Show efficiency, objectivity, logic. Offer options.

- *Friend:* Relaxed but unsure, emotional, not a risk-taker
  Give personal attention, be convincing, offer friendship and "family talk."

- *Controller:* Disciplined, cool, controlled, shows no emotions.
  Give facts, figures, proof. Avoid idle talk.

- *Actor:* Talkative, excited, emotional, impulsive, persuasive; permanently acting.
  Show admiration. Be an audience. Make the actor feel special with offers or by flattery.

- *Aggressor:* Distrustful, offensive by nature; attacks without reason.
  Deal with patience; don't argue, don't defend, ignore offense. Wait until he or she is out of steam, then make a factual proposal.

Of course, not everyone is a prototype. But good observation can help you find the most suitable style to adopt.

The Press

The press can be an important channel of communication for stating a position and selling an image or an idea. When you are interviewed, make sure the reporter gets the facts straight. It helps the reporter, and it helps you even more. It is in your best interest. Another golden rule is not to be defensive or boastful. It does not go down well with the press. Give in writing whatever you can.

Preparation

Whether negotiating, interviewing, or meeting with someone, prepare yourself in advance. Think over your position; what to say, what is involved. Weigh the consequences. It will save you from mistakes.

CHECKLIST

- Do you adapt your style to the people you negotiate with?

- Are you conscious of your own behavior? Your own vulnerability?

- Do you prepare yourself thoroughly?

It is to your advantage to speak the language of the other party.

MEETINGS

Meetings are a form of communication. They can also be frustrating time-wasters. The results often don't justify the hourly cost of the participants, the rental of meeting rooms, preparation, and follow-up; the graphics and the minutes or the secretarial work. The biggest waste is time that management could put to better use.

How to Make Meetings Better

Eliminate meetings? By no means! Meetings with real purpose, whose participants are well-prepared and directly involved, are useful and necessary. Here are five tips to help you avoid meetings that waste everyone's time:

1. **Call only meetings that have a clear purpose.** Avoid routine meetings with no real meaning (because it's Thursday or the second Tuesday of the month). Better to use the extra time to visit clients.

2. **Prepare a clear agenda.** Don't use the word "various"—this usually stands for various ways to lose time.

3. **Start on time and stay on time.** Fix the duration of the meeting beforehand. Limiting the time reduces idle discussion. Use time pressure to reach decisions. More time does not produce better decisions.

4. **Prepare concise, telegraphic-style minutes.** Distribute them promptly.

5. **Make sure everyone knows the rules.** Include time allotted to speakers, deadlines, responsibilities, and follow-up.

	Type of meeting	
	Presentation/ Information	**Recommendation/ Decision**
Size of group	maximum	minimum
Emphasis	presentation/ understanding	discussion/conclusion
Preparation	Lecturer/speaker	all participants
Information base/distribution of material	before/during/after	before
Significant data and facts	presented	"on the table" prior to the debate
Discussion/ questions	to clear doubts; questions at the end • no interruptions • answer may come as the presentation proceeds.	dissent is good; argue, consider, and reconcile opinions; set deadline

Figure 4. Guidelines for Efficient Meetings

The purpose of meetings, generally, is to present information (presentation, information-sharing) or to make decisions (consensus-seeking). Figure 4 offers some guidelines on how to structure both types of meetings.

A GOOD LEADER

Meetings need a chairman, a leader, or a facilitator. A good leader

- creates a participative climate
- minimizes conflicts, but encourages free flow of ideas

- guides to reach consensus
- sticks to the agenda and time frame

A GOOD PARTICIPANT

For decision-making, a good participant

- is well-prepared
- listens to the discussion
- contributes his or her ideas
- influences deliberations by talking assertively, but briefly

Unstructured Meetings

A deliberately unstructured meeting becomes, in essence, a brainstorming process. They are best held outside the office in an informal environment: relaxed, uninhibited, letting imagination take a free ride, never ridiculing later for ideas that might seem absurd in a suit and tie. Brainstorming produces the most creative ideas—imaginative, unusual, at times crazy, original, and different.

CHECKLIST

- Make sure meetings are results-oriented and have a real purpose.
- Don't waste time and money. Be prepared and follow-up.
- Critique the last five meetings you attended. How many were productive?
- How could you make the next ones more productive?

Meetings are a time investment. Investments need payout.

MAKING A PRESENTATION

Some do's and don'ts:

1. **Prepare with care.** Think through what you will say. Put yourself in the shoes of your audience. How familiar are they with your subject? Are they interested in learning? How much detail should you include?

2. **Make eye contact.** Look at the people in the audience when you speak.

3. **Be enthusiastic.** Motivate your audience with strong opening and closing statements.

4. **Speak to the audience.** You may glance at notes so you don't skip subjects, but don't prepare sentences to read or repeat from memory.

5. **Use graphics.** Graphs show more than verbal explanations; visual aids are always helpful. But don't read numbers or text from a transparency. Point out what's relevant, for example, the order of magnitude, not the cents.

6. **Speak clearly and convincingly.** Stick to your presentation. Don't deviate. Keep it simple and avoid jargon.

7. **Don't volunteer information.** Respond to relevant questions, then keep going.

8. **Don't guess if you don't have the answer.** Say you will check or confirm when appropriate to do so.

9. **Time is money.** Go fast. Check time. Skip details. Slow down when asked.

10. **Be honest and forthcoming.** Point out achievements. Assume responsibility for failures. Give credit to your group. Don't blame others. Attack issues, not people.

11. **Be believable.** Excess optimism marks you as a dreamer. Pessimism marks you as a "has been." Be realistic. Watch reactions—they may tell you something.

12. **Don't hide problems.** Explain how you will solve them.

13. **Don't be cynical.** Never belittle your company, your efforts, or the competition.

14. **Try to get feedback.** Reaction from others may be different from your impressions.

The leader (the boss) wants to "feel" competence and good judgment from you. He or she will question and provoke you: Who will solve the problem and how? What if? Why? When? Nothing is taken for granted. The boss will notice when answers are evasive; when hopes replace action plans; when competition is blamed for bad results.

CHECKLIST

- Never be defensive. Be positive and factual.
- Match problems with solutions.
- Offer alternatives, but have your own recommendation ready.

A presentation provides visibility. It's a career opportunity, don't waste it!

5

LEADERS ARE TEAMBUILDERS

Any collection of people can form a group—a group of tourists, a group of spectators, a management group. Management groups usually call themselves management teams. Often, they are only groups. But it's a basketball *team* that wins the medal; a surgical *team* that performs an operation. You don't hear of basketball or soccer groups.

A group is unrelated (tourist), uncoordinated (spectators), or under a traditional hierarchical system (management). A team operates with skilled coordination. Its members share common goals and values. They are mutually supportive. They work together and communicate regularly. They actively participate. There is a strong sense of common purpose and consensus-seeking.

WHY A TEAM?

No leader has all the skills. The skills a team has complement those of the leader. Combining complementary skills capitalizes on the natural formation of groups, turning them into teams. A successful team is a portrait of diversity: diverse professional backgrounds, experience, temperament, intelligence, behavior, extroversion, introversion, dominance, emotional stability. People with identical ideas and reactions, "yes-men," or just clever people won't make a good team.

By forming his or her team(s), a leader replaces individualistic, competitive management style with a more trusting and cooperative style. Selection is most important. Without the right people nothing is possible.

What Are the Advantages of a Team?

- Input of many people of diverse skills

- Getting the best out of each other

- Diverse experience, knowledge, and judgment

- Not dependent on any individual (accident, transfer, retirement)

- Self-regeneration by recruitment

- Passing experience to new members

What Makes a Team?

CLIMATE:

- Mutual trust and cooperation

- Openness and reciprocal support

- Disagreement without conflict

- Elimination of status differences

- Leveling of human differences

CHARACTERISTICS:

- Mixed composition of 6 to 9 people

- Regular face-to-face meetings with frequent interaction

- No 'us' and 'them'

- Clear purpose, commitment, and identification with each other

- Structured and divergent, but disciplined

- Mutual care among team players, with a will to do the job well so others can do theirs

Figure 5. Different Instruments—Same Music

To harmonize all instruments, the orchestra needs a conductor. Teams also need a conductor—a leader—to coordinate, resolve conflicts, and unite the team to a common purpose. It requires great interpersonal skill. Leading a team is a good experience, a stepping stone to higher leadership.

TYPES OF TEAMS

Some teams are permanent. For example, management teams are permanent. So are planning and product development teams, among others. A management team supports the leader. The members participate in major decisions and strive for best results by joint effort. Planning, development, and other teams are pools of diverse talent. Participation is part time in addition to other functions, or in some cases, full time.

Other teams are temporary. Temporary teams are formed when the existing organization cannot develop an important project or resolve a major problem, in spite of available talent. Such *ad hoc,* or "tiger teams" concentrate the full-time brainpower of a selected few to resolve a specific problem or complete a project within a limited time frame.

Members are from different departments; usually they are temporarily relieved from their regular duties to dedicate all their time to the team effort. The temporary delegation of team members' regular functions should be looked upon as a test and opportunity for the "title holder" and the temporary replacement.

If the team succeeds, the visibility and prestige of team members will increase. If it fails, the team disbands and reputations may suffer. Yet, smart people learn from mistakes and can regain prestige fast. In any case, membership appeals to ambitious individuals. Those who aren't risk-takers shy away, helping natural selection. Equally important is that the team or its spokesperson has access to the highest local authority to present its results. Lack of direct contact can be demotivating.

TEAM PROFILE

Composing a good team is a complex task. After years of study, Dr. Meredith Belbin designed a nearly ideal composition.[5] Players assume their "roles" unknowingly. The doer, the skeptic, the organizer, the natural leader, introverts, and extroverts. Each contributes to the team's success. The basic characteristics tested by Dr. Belbin were:

- intelligence

- dominance

- extroversion/introversion

- stability/anxiety

For his eight-person teams, Dr. Belbin identified four outward-looking types, concerned with the world outside the team, and four inward-looking types, mainly concerned with the team itself.

Outward-Looking

- *Coordinator (Chairman):* Strong, realistic, disciplined, dominant, extroverted. Not brilliant, but creative.

- *Task leader (Shaper):* Self-confident, extroverted, emotional, impatient, strong drive.

- *Idea originator (Plant):* Highest I.Q., highly creative, introverted, dominant, critical, moody.

- *Ambassador (Resource investigator):* Brings new ideas and information from outside; stable, sociable, extroverted, enthusiastic, diplomatic.

Inward-Looking

- *Executor (Company worker):* Turns strategies into tasks. Stable, controlled, organizer, disciplined, competitive.

- *Critic, analyst (Monitor or evaluator):* High I.Q., extroverted, stable, dispassionate, clear judgment.

- *Team mother (Team worker):* Stable, extroverted, "confessor," sensitive, popular, good listener.

- *Controller (Finisher):* Assumes all follow-ups. Anxious, introverted, fussy, checks details and deadlines, sense of duty and urgency.

Note: The titles in parentheses are Dr. Belbin's original ones.

In practice, two or more "roles" may be combined. Even so, it's hard to form an ideal team. It's important to note that the emphasis is on harmonizing diverse ideas of opposing characters and temperaments into consensus solution. This is a long way from the situation in which the boss is receptive to opinions only if they coincide with his or her views.

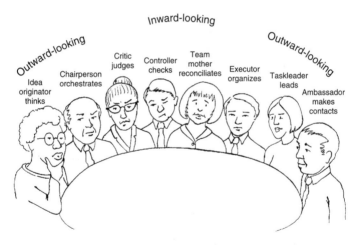

Figure 6. The Dream Team

Perceiving and Judging

Another classification useful for forming teams is from Carl Jung, founder of analytical psychology. It classifies people into those who mainly perceive by sense or intuition and those who judge by thinking and feeling.

- *Sensor:* Acts on highly developed senses; tries to understand the problem; digs up facts, feels what needs to be done.

- *Intuitor:* Looks at the big picture, beyond what's visible; avoids detail, is creative; finds patterns and relationships others don't see; anticipates problems.

- *Thinker:* Analyzes, is logical; organizes, fights for his or her convictions; is fair and objective.

- *Feeler:* Is humanistic, likes harmony, helps others; rouses enthusiasm; seeks consensus; is a peacemaker.

Using either classification as a guide helps to identify and bring together a good mixture of personalities.

In spite of all valid arguments in favor of consensus-seeking teams, a warning is due. A delayed decision may be a decision too late. Team members must avoid endless discussions and reach decisions fast. A saying by Napoleon comes to mind: "Let me fight a coalition...." When circumstances require, a leader will make important decisions without consulting the team.

CHECKLIST

- Did you identify which role you play on the team? Your teammates' roles?

- Is your team composed of people with diverse talent, bonded by common purpose?

- Are you a good team player? Willing to give team objectives priority over personal interest?

You can't make a good soccer team out of the eleven best goalkeepers. You need good players of different skills.

"There is no limit to what a man can do, or where he can go, if he doesn't mind who gets the credit." (On Gorbachev's old desk in the Kremlin)

6

LEADERS PLAN

In the sixties, strategic planning was *the* road to success. Now some managers think that it's overrated. In a world of rapid change, are plans of any real value? Today's solutions could be tomorrow's mistake. So why plan at all?

For the skeptics, here's a remark by General (later President) Dwight Eisenhower: "Plans are useless, but planning is essential." I'd rather say that "planning is essential, but under rapidly changing scenarios, rigid plans become useless." The process of planning clears the mind. The plan creates purpose. Planning cannot foretell the future, but as trends develop, it serves as a basis to build on. Errors occur, surprises happen. For example, a given consumer trend could take an unexpected turn. Remember the famous wrong forecasts: that the price of oil would reach $100 a barrel by the end of the '80s; or that horse manure would cover the streets of London (but then came the motor car). But this is not the rule.

Most trends are helpful guides. Take demographic growth, for example. The combination of facts and trends permits us to create different scenarios, from the most likely to the least expected. Plans follow the most likely scenario, with enough built-in flexibility to adjust to new realities. No building is constructed without a plan. No trial lawyer goes to court without a strategy. No business can be successful without both.

It is important to remember:

- Planning is thinking and rethinking the business. It is not filling in forms.

- Today, planning is even more vital than ever. Risk appears to increase faster than opportunity. We now need more information and more creativity to find the best solution.

Staying successful requires courage to change direction. To dump, when necessary, a major strength of the past. To adapt quickly to new situations. Those who don't plan ahead fall behind. Organizations can't live on past successes; sticking to their old ways, their old procedures, their old products. Past success offers no guarantee of continuity without planning, thinking ahead, and anticipating change. Many big organizations learned this lesson by bitter experience. If you miss the train, the distance between those on board and you—still on the platform—increases fast.

THE PLANNING PROCESS

Planning begins with a review of all aspects of the business. Evaluating strengths and weaknesses; competitive and market position; new trends; technical developments; human and material resources. Strategy is built on awareness, then summarized in the strategic plan, or business plan. The budget, or financial plan, can then be prepared.

Strategy is the organization of objectives to obtain advantage by being better than the competition. There are choices between the *or* and *and* of apparently contradictory goals. Which offers better perspectives? Diversification or

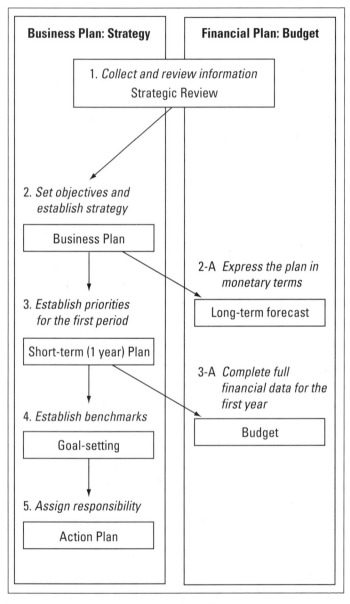

Figure 7. Planning Strategy and Budgets

concentration of efforts? Lowest cost or highest quality? Could it be both? Answers to theses questions develop as the plan is being prepared.

As substitutes for plans, budgets are useless. Too many financial projections are based on the present, plus wishful improvements in volume, cost, and price. Hoped-for financial results replace goals, without strategy and tactics to get there. Such plans are like fixing the score before the game without directions on how to achieve it.

Planning is not a once-a-year event restricted to specific functions. It's a continuous process. Planning involves the input of as many people as practical for information and ideas. Macroeconomic projections may have to come from an economist, but the front line (from sales person to operator) is equally important. No

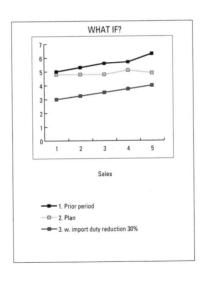

Figure 8. Graphics Are a Good Way to Present Multiple Plans

one knows more on a given topic than the people who deal with it and live with it. Their input is fundamental.

Good planning does not rely on one set of numbers. Different scenarios are projected, explained, and ranked by probability, and the most likely is chosen for the plan. Different scenarios are based on (see Figure 8):

- what if? (a possible event with major bearing on the business)
- high-medium-low projection
- alternate methods of evaluation

Developing scenarios helps contingency planning. With proper benchmarks, red flags indicate needed action.

Strategic Planning

Strategic planning is preceded by preparing and organizing all available information on the economy, markets, and products. It includes raw materials, technical developments, human resources planning, and financing.

Competitive position is among the most important information: uniqueness, advantage, parity, and disadvantage (in products, cost, quality, research, human resources, and so on). Special emphasis is on:

- *Clients* (target clients, customers decision making, preferences, plans, market penetration)
- *Competitors* (finances, marketing, technical & management strength, plans, philosophy, reputation)
- *Cost*

Preparation and appraisal of the plan are based on this data. Fundamental to the process are:

- good intelligence
- information analysis—focusing on the whole, not missing any detail.
- reasoned assumptions vs. historical trends
- creativity in planning—looking at things in a novel way
- using, but not blindfolded by, past experience
- consideration of change as an opportunity

It is irrelevant whether planning takes place in the boardroom or through informal discussions. What matters is the process—reviewing and debating issues, and commitment to the final plan.

The Business Plan

The business plan covers corporate objectives (when/where) and strategy (how). The details of the business plan establish goals and strategy for each segment, department, and activity.

Goals must be consistent and demanding, but achievable. Departmental goals, which fit into corporate objectives, are as a rule, more specific.

Goals	Action Plan (Responsible)
• Reduce working capital to X days' sales.	• Operations manager, 2nd quarter
• Launch 3 new consumer products.	• Marketing director, one per quarter
• Reduce delivery time from Y to Z days.	• Operations manager, mid-year
• Start recycling waste and eliminate buildup.	• Plant manager, October

Action plans are the implementation of goals and determine who is responsible and when to take action.

Here are some examples:

The Short-Term Plan

The *short-term plan* covers the first period of the business plan. *Goals* and *action plans* are partial solutions toward long-term objectives. For example, suppose strategy calls for market dominance for a certain product within three years by introducing quality guarantee, five-day delivery, and so on. Implementing this strategy may take three years, following various steps:

- *Short-term plan (first year):* The goal is to equal the competitor's market share.

- *Second year:* To achieve at least 30% of total market share.

- *Third year:* To reach 35% share and launch second product.

The strategic planning process, as described, may be too proceduralized for small operations or the highly advanced ones. In such organizations:

- Goals are developed through informal contacts and are known by all

- Access to information is open and unrestricted.

- Teamwork replaces action plans; it's "us" and "now," with no need to establish time limits and responsibility.

For the great majority of organizations, however, a formal approach is needed.

CHECKLIST

- Gather business intelligence. Collect all pertinent information from all sources all the time.

- Formulate strategy and objectives. Use resources (knowledge!) and strengths to your best advantage.

- Set measurable short- and long-term goals, including how, when, and by whom.

A rigid plan is taking the right road, but ignoring the detour sign.

7

EFFICIENCY LEADERS

Global competition forces cost reduction to be a permanent priority. Price is not determined by cost any longer. Allowable cost depends on achievable price and surviving on cost reduction. Successful companies offer the highest value at the lowest cost in the shortest response time.

Among the many ways to reduce cost, the simplistic ones are the most popular. Reducing numerical headcount to make the organization "mean and lean" more often leaves it weak and demoralized. Reducing certain expenses may claim immediate savings, but the damage appears later. While profit improvements are reported regularly, deteriorations remain buried. Then come more reports on "savings." Most such measures don't succeed in long-run profit improvement.

Saving on payroll and limiting headcount are necessary, but measures must be planned. Reengineer before you cut headcount or scrap R&D or advertising. Use resources better; be more efficient. Quoting Benjamin Disraeli, "There can be no economy where there is no efficiency."

SEEING THE OPPORTUNITY IN COST

During the '80s, nonquality, cost-generating functions rose more than productive ones—more reports and controls, more control of controls. Bureaucracy that adds no value is a real "organosaurus." This is changing.

Cost can be analyzed in the conventional way or by opportunity:

Principal cost elements		**Opportunities**
• employment cost	=	procedures and productivity
• material cost	=	quality
• capital, equipment, and process cost	=	time

EMPLOYMENT COST

Employment cost depends on procedures and productivity—on industrial engineering as much as on human resources management or salary levels. Opportunities are in:

- untangled, simple procedures
- fewer layers; empowerment
- no excessive controls
- verbal communication; less paper
- shared targets and responsibilities
- permanent training

The result is good employee morale, efficient operation, and higher productivity. In financial terms—lower employment cost.

MATERIAL COST

Material cost depends on quality: eliminating rejects, rework, and waste and fully enforcing high standards—

"Do it right in the first place." Ensure quality in all activities, at all levels. The customer is royalty; the supplier is a partner in developing the best product at the lowest price. The benefit is mutual. Management and employees share pride in quality and service. In financial terms: lower material cost (no waste and rework), better selling price, and higher volume (customer satisfaction).

EQUIPMENT, WORKING CAPITAL, AND PROCESS COST

Equipment, working capital, and process cost are controlled by cycle time. Acquire more efficient equipment, or develop or buy new technologies or processes. But the biggest saving is in reducing total process time—elapsed time between receipt of raw material and delivery of finished product. A faster process (new machine) does the trick only if it eliminates a bottleneck.

Faster flow requires:

- good scheduling and removing bottlenecks
- changing layout, products, and processes
- good maintenance
- employee participation
- suppliers' cooperation
- Eliminating bureaucratic and process restraints

Financial gains are:

- lower inventories = less working capital
- less space required = lower investment
- faster deliveries = faster repeat orders and faster collection

An alternative to higher volume is focused operation. Cut down on products and services that consume excessive (process) time; have low machine-to-people utilization; obstruct fast flow; and are outside the core business. Avoid, if possible, bulk and special products under the same roof, same management. The two need different handling.

REENGINEERING

A concept known as business process reengineering replaces downsizing by a zero-based study of all processes, systems, and products.[6] The reengineering team identifies processes (manufacturing, marketing, administrative, and so on), then redesigns each, starting from scratch, as if they never existed. It's best done by multifunctional teams, with members from production, engineering, marketing, administration, or other departments, according to the business. Success depends on the willingness to abandon, not just modify, a failing system. For example (from the world of politics): Gorbachev tried to improve and save a bankrupt system. Yeltsin scrapped the system and started from scratch.

Reengineering *rethinks* the business from A to Z:

- It identifies the purpose of the business
- It forms a strategy, once the mission is clear
- It builds on strength and eliminates causes for weakness (improves or withdraws them)
- It concentrates on the core business
- It considers outsourcing products or services, if cheaper or better.

TIME, QUALITY, AND SIMPLIFICATION

With the reengineering done and the tactics established, it's essential to remain fully committed, and implement the plan stepwise.

Suggested procedures and priorities are listed below:

- Time as measure achieves:

  ➤ lower cost through faster processes and lower working capital

  ➤ customer satisfaction through faster response time

  ➤ innovation through faster development and launching of new products

- Quality for excellence achieves:

  ➤ lower cost by elimination of waste and re-work

  ➤ customer satisfaction by better value for money

  ➤ high employee morale through commitment to excellence

- Simplification for efficiency achieves

  ➤ lower cost through simplified procedures

  ➤ faster decisions through empowerment and fewer layers

  ➤ competitive advantage through simpler and better products

  ➤ creativity and innovation through informal environment

CHECKLIST

- Simplify to gain efficiency over bureaucracy.
- Set high standards of quality to reach excellence.
- Create an environment for innovation to lead.

The customer is the final judge of delivery, cost, and price.

8

CHANGE LEADERS

The success of an organization depends increasingly on its ability to adjust quickly to new situations. New trends, regulations, and fierce competition force companies to make major organizational changes in order to remain competitive. The cost in management time and money is significant. Often, an even higher price is paid in employee morale and failures. Thus, companies must justify change—it must be beneficial for the company and its constituencies.

Equally important is timing. It reflects on the vision of the leader. Too often, the company makes the change too late—after they start losing money, market, and cash flow, and funds for the necessary investment are no longer available. A good leader starts change when it's still sunny and the first clouds are far away. Good reasons and good timing still cannot guarantee immunity from pitfalls, such as employee resistance, confusion, and excessive cost.

TIPS FOR SUCCESS

This chapter presents seven considerations that can make justified changes a success.

Careful Planning

Careful planning saves time and money. Chances for success improve with a well-prepared disclosure and good communication; with careful weighing of potential resistance and its consequences; with a detailed timetable for execution.

Motivation

Employee resistance is often self-defense, and fear of losing security, power, or status. To offset such fears discuss potential new career paths, the necessity and advantages of a different position, the reasons for the change; and show appreciation for loyalty.

Some employees lack self-confidence and consider any change a threat. They are afraid to cope with new responsibilities, another boss, or different colleagues. Patience is needed to explain and convince. Teaching, training, and full support are good remedies.

Communication

Good communication is vital. Reasons for the change must be explained beforehand. Clear communication is the best investment, since resistance is often due to misinterpretations, half-information, and rumors that precede the change. Easy-to-understand written and verbal communication should reach all layers.

Salesmanship may be necessary to "sell" a major change. Be persuasive, but honest, in promoting the concept. Misleading sales talk has a boomerang effect.

Involvement

Employee involvement during the planning stage has two advantages:

- To learn from the experience of people on the job. Employee involvement prevents mistakes and wrong assessments—and expensive consequences. Those affected by the change can usually provide the best insight, but their objectivity must be scrutinized.

• The sooner people are involved in the plan, the more they become involved. Those on board early are supportive and spread the word. This prevents rumors and the build-up of resistance.

When people get seriously involved, the situation becomes easier. It's not "us" and "them" (management). A well-justified change becomes everybody's project, not just management's. The motto is "We, the company, will benefit from the change."

Trust

Another great facilitator is trust. Credibility of management, based on past experience plays a key role. Where trust is lacking, problems multiply. The best remedy is honest information and better communication. These are stepping stones to future trust.

Contingencies

In spite of the best efforts, some resistance may remain. If the problem is wage loss, negotiation is necessary. In other situations, leaders of the resistance and their motivation have to be identified. If direct communication does not resolve the problem, negotiation, co-option, and, in extreme cases, coercion may be justified.

Execution

Once everything is prepared and in place, execution should be fast. A D-day must be set to introduce the new organization. Postponement is not recommended, even if there is a last-minute problem.

Over 100 years ago, Benjamin Disraeli said: "Change is inevitable. In a progressive country change is constant." The same can be said for business.

CHECKLIST

- Organizational changes must be well thought out to justify cost and risk.
- Success depends on communication, motivation, education, and involvement.
- Sources and strength of resistance must be anticipated. Deal with potential problems from the early stages on.

Coherence of management and trust in leadership eliminate opposition and tip the balance in favor of renewal.

9

LEADERS MAKE DECISIONS, SOLVE PROBLEMS, USE EXPERIENCE

DECISION MAKING

There is some truth in the saying that a bad decision is better than no decision. Mistakes usually can be corrected. Few things are as harmful as letting things ride or leaving questions unanswered until time resolves them. There may be an occasional exception. But slow decisions work as a brake. Their effect on business is negative. Rush decisions are equally bad.

But, rule-of-thumb decisions often lack objectivity, being influenced by emotions, past experience, surroundings, and personality. Decisions on the same issue may vary if made by engineers or accountants; logical thinkers or idea people; doers or detail-oriented people; young or old.

Good decisions require facts and judgment. Quality of judgment depends on intuition, experience, and mental discipline. Question perceptions. Consider alternatives and consequences. Before deciding:

- Ask yourself pertinent questions.
- List your options.
- Evaluate each option.

- Construct best and worst scenarios.
- Judge probabilities of success.
- Judge consequences of failure.
- Be decisive. There is no decision without risk.

We need to question the potential biases and subjective factors in individual perception. These can be internal or external:

- *Internal:* Personality traits can influence a decision. Am I looking at the problem objectively, or am I influenced emotionally? Are my decisions influenced by likes and dislikes, unpleasant experience, beliefs?

- *External:* Environment can impact a decision. Am I under pressure by the media or public opinion? From colleagues, "experts," trends? Do I have objective, factual data on hand before I decide?

Much depends on the weight of the decision. Small decisions are fast. Bigger decisions need facts and judgment. For complex decisions, cross-functional problem-solving teams may offer the best solution (see Chapter 5). A team can assist a doer who is too impatient to analyze a problem thoroughly enough to make the detailed diagnosis prior to decision. In most instances, simple gut feeling won't stand up against reliable data.

One has to bear in mind that management is an art, not a science. Few management problems can be quantified to solve with formulas. Self-analysis, questioning, and judgment must complement analysis of facts and knowledge. Under all circumstances, it's necessary to sort out what's important from what's not. Don't rearrange the deck chairs on the Titanic.

Will what seems important today be important tomorrow? A week from now? A month or year from now? What will be more important? Ask yourself these questions before deciding. Learn to choose your priorities objectively.

CHECKLIST

- In decision making, importance must have priority over quantity or even urgency.
- Decisions must be fast, yet well thought out.
- Intuition, facts, and questioning are essential to making the right decisions.

The art of management is mixing ingredients in correct proportion: intuition, rational analysis of data, and that extra drop of risk-taking that gives the flavor.

NEGOTIATING AND PROBLEM SOLVING

Resolving problems often requires negotiation. People negotiate to win. A concession, a discount, forgiveness, or a promotion. Children negotiate for candy, youngsters to attend a football game. The negotiation can be friendly or become a power struggle. It can end in mutual satisfaction (win-win), a compromise, or becoming enemies forever (lose-lose).

A problem-solving negotiation should never end in war, but in finding mutually agreeable solutions. The parties negotiate in defense of their interests without aiming to destroy each other.

Methods for obtaining desired results are different for problem solving and resolving power struggles. A good negotiator has the same characteristics in both instances. Good negotiators

- collect, check, and probe for information
- know as much about the other person as possible
- are skilled at observing people and their reactions

- have their facts straight and have thought through their plans
- are patient and tolerate conflict and ambiguity
- have sound business judgment
- know the bottom line for concessions
- listen and communicate well
- are open-minded
- have a "poker face"
- distinguish issues from people

The difference in the attitude of negotiators, whether the target is to win at all cost, or to find a mutually satisfactory solution is shown below:

Problem solving (win-win) and partnering	**Hard bargaining (win-lose)**
• builds trust; shows positive feelings	• intimidates; uses maximum power
• minimizes differences	• overstates demands
• is predictable; no hidden cards	• plays games; is ambiguous
• is clear and logical	• confuses
• is conciliatory, creative	• threatens
• is relaxed, shows patience	• shows anger, hostility
• is flexible	• is inflexible
• seeks common interest	• fights for every small advantage
• builds interdependence	• forces independence
• makes others comfortable	• harasses
• yields to good alternatives	• yields to pressure

A good negotiator resolves a problem to mutual satisfaction, in a climate of confidence. He or she integrates viewpoints, dealing equal to equal. No one loses. In the end, everyone feels satisfied with the accomplishment—everyone wins.

CHECKLIST

- Can we solve the problem without conflict?
- Can my view of the other party be wrong?
- Can an approach in good faith result in a good solution?

A war has winners and losers. Mainly losers. A good agreement makes good friends.

EXPERIENCE

By conventional wisdom, experience is "it." Another school of thought argues that experience is an obstacle—it prevents new approaches and fresh ideas; it hinders creativity and blocks the mind. Actually, the answer lies in the interplay of experience and creativity. Evolution finds its source in experience, inventions in creativity. Experience and creativity are complementary.

Without experience, driving a car, flying an airplane, or handling any complex situation, is a sure disaster. Model Ts were a breakthrough and major step in the development of the modern automobile. Yet they are unsuitable for today's highways. All products were once new and original—some even revolutionary. A few were rejected at first. Was experience to blame? People who place little value on experience might think so. Yet, without experience-based knowledge, few new ideas are born.

An old chair breaks. If your hobby is carpentry, with experience alone, you can build a copy. With experience and imagination, you can build a better and nicer chair. But with imagination and no experience, who knows what you will build? A solid tree trunk? A board fastened to the ceiling? An unsteady lap? The solution may be sensational, but rarely is. Most progress comes from experience-based evolution.

Experience must be used with care. It should enhance the vision. The danger is habit—difficult to break. Habits must not stand in the way of creativity, intellectual courage and boldness of mind. So use experience and change habits. Change and improve ways of doing things. Abandon old approaches and past solutions. Look at the world from a different angle!

Experience is a basic reference, not *the* truth. It helps prevent mistakes. A creative mind uses experience to search for and create new ways.

CHECKLIST

- There is no sound judgment without experience.

- Experience gives insight. Habit accommodates.

- Creativity is imagination over habits.

Experience is your personal memory bank. It's how you use it that makes the difference.

10

TREND LEADERS

The *Checklist for Leaders* would not be complete without a summary of major trends.

MANAGEMENT BY OBJECTIVES

Management by Objectives (MBO) was the first comprehensive modern management concept. It represented the final break with Taylor's rigid hierarchy of thinkers and doers and supervised mass production. MBO is still useful, emphasizing both *management* (style) and *objectives* (results). Goals are to be reached; performance measured. MBO focuses on *what to do* rather than *how to do it*—on objectives rather than activities—work, not busyness. There is strong orientation to results, even in staff functions. Style is participative, with delegation of authority and team work. Common objectives are the catalyst. Creativity, innovation, and consumer orientation are emphasized. So is information and feedback. The challenge and personal commitment are to setting and reaching goals.

MBO is not a technique. Like its later cousin TQM, it's a philosophy, a mental attitude that is logical in objectives and humanistic in approach. Education and training must precede implementation.

The aim of MBO is improved performance by planning and doing the right things at lowest cost.

TOTAL QUALITY MANAGEMENT

Total Quality Management (TQM) is a more recent trend leader. It's here to stay. TQM's great merit is the amplitude of sound concepts under one lead idea: *excellence.*

TQM, as Dr. Edwards Deming conceived it, started as a quality system based on statistical process control. It soon turned into a comprehensive philosophy that incorporated the best of MBO, just-in-time, and other methods. Its principal thrust is quality. Everything is quality—not just products and service, but behavior too. Management is quality, and so is the voice and courtesy of the phone operator.

TQM is quality in all activities: technical, commercial, administrative, and human—everything that makes cost and quality competitive. Focusing on quality, says Deming, improves productivity, customer satisfaction, better employee morale, innovation, and higher profits. Key words are prevention, not correction; *continuous improvement* (Kaizen) through training and commitment; *total customer satisfaction;* and *people orientation.* It is the search for the best in everything.

With such powerful appeal, why then is TQM not always a success? Why do some companies never achieve the final goal of gaining long-term competitive advantage? Here are some reasons:

- TQM is not a pushbutton process. Introducing TQM requires a profound cultural change and extraordinary persistence. It's a long, difficult process. The biggest challenge is to change human behavior, which requires full reeducation and much training.

- Some managers enthusiastically support TQM, but are unaware that they too must change— that they must delegate and empower.

- A common error is excessive concentration on form rather than essence—measuring activity (time spent), not results.

- Another cause for failure is introducing TQM as a parallel system. To work, TQM must become one with strategy; the culture of the organization must adapt.

- Probably most failures are due to the lack of commitment by top management. Management often buys the package on TQM know-how, then leaves implementation to second and third layers. They could just as well save the expense. Without full, enthusiastic participation of top management, TQM does not work.

PROCESS REENGINEERING

Process reengineering rethinks how to create value for the customer—how to manufacture and sell the product or service. It provides the ultimate answer, by starting from scratch and taking a fresh, unbiased approach. Reengineering involves a major cultural change. It's a complex, often dramatic, process.

Business process reengineering can result in downsizing, which can be done in one or several steps. There is a danger though, that downsizing itself becomes the goal. It's important to reduce costs. But to be successful, a company has to create value. Savings alone are not sufficient. Downsizing and outsourcing may be fundamental, but without other measures a company cannot be successful.

Success depends on strategy and a vision of the future, not on short-term results only. Work toward long-term goals. Strategy, as well as process, must be subject to reengineering or reinventing.

To gain competitive advantage, successful companies, as successful leaders, often choose the unconventional.

Companies do so in products and markets, in alliances with rivals, by new approaches and other means. Successful companies are creative, not downsizers only.

Another long-term danger in excessive downsizing is burning out the "survivors" by stretching their workloads to the limit. Yet the remaining workforce is essential to future success. (More on this later.)

WHICH TO CHOOSE?

How do you develop the best strategies and processes for your organization? Consider your needs. Listen to different ideas. Draw a plan that fits, go with it, and stay committed.

By different approaches, the highways of MBO, TQM, and reengineering sometimes run parallel and sometimes intersect. The final goal is similar: to gain long-term competitive advantage, not to resolve specific problems.

BENCHMARKING

Benchmarking involves searching for the best in all fields, among all companies. It targets specific areas, to discover how someone does something better. The Japanese call it *dantotsu*—striving to become the best of the best. Benchmarking investigates all kinds of companies, not just competitors. Look for those companies that use a better (the best) method in manufacturing, accounting, training, product promotion, or other fields. It's recognizing that improvements can be made by learning from the experience of others.

Benchmarking can be divided into three types:

- *Intercompany benchmarking* analyzes the best performance in a given function and applies it in all other departments and affiliates.

- *Business-based benchmarking* studies what the competition does better, and why.

- *Functional benchmarking* searches among all companies, anywhere, for the best performer in a given function, to see how it's done.

The goal is to become the best by living up to the best in every field. Disassembling a competitive model, as done in the car industry, is a benchmark activity. In a different form, so is management consulting.

The *target,* that is, the *best,* is generally identified through client interviews, trade magazines, and other sources. After studying the function, the benchmarking company applies the better methods in its operations.

A common error in business-based benchmarking is targeting the old rival rather than the new and upcoming competitors who may have newer ideas.

OTHER TRENDS

There are new trends in all areas—in human resources, the factory floor, finance, and in corporate organization.

Peter Drucker, in a magazine interview,[7] emphasized three points, among others:

- Bosses must learn to look at other employees as colleagues, not as subordinates.

- Where teamwork is encouraged, differentiated individual performance bonuses are counter-productive.

- Intrapreneurship functions only where innovation is continuous and supported by the entire administration. Innovators rebelling against bureaucracy won't succeed.

The second point, performance-related pay (PRP), is the most controversial point. It has become popular worldwide, following the trend of participative management, empowerment, and entrepreneurship. PRP is an incentive for initiative and good performance that benefits both company and employees. In addition, by setting goals, a company can direct efforts toward one or several priorities: quality, new products, reorganization, accident prevention, and so on.

Implementing PRP too quickly has provoked growing criticism, based on:

- the difficulty of objective measure
- the tendency to reward routine
- time lost in inventing the incentives
- questioning the value of money as a motivator
- the contradiction between team spirit and individual incentives

Possible solutions are to:

- Establish clear, easy-to-control quality objectives.
- Reward group, rather than individual, performance.
- Combine material reward with other forms of recognition.
- Most important, avoid objectives that discourage risk-taking and creativity.

Inverse Evaluation

Another system gaining acceptance in the Human Resources area is *inverse evaluation*. Employees evaluate their bosses. This is usually done by answering a professionally prepared questionnaire, and signing it, or not. Then the boss meets face to face with the group to discuss major criticisms. At the end, the boss has to decide on his or her own improvement plan. The details vary, but the beginning is always hard. Where culture permits, however, it's a useful tool.

Diminishing Employee Loyalty

A recent negative trend is diminishing employee loyalty. Declining loyalty is a response to reorganization forced upon companies by fierce competition. The way a company handles cutbacks determines much about the loyalty and trust of the survivors. A frequent error, committed even by companies that handle dismissals in an exemplary way, is to forget about the survivors. Many of them are traumatized, too, and need special attention. The solutions are communication, transparency, involvement, and human contact. Only clear explanations of the measures taken and future plans restore trust. Proof that the strategy works motivates people.

Clear and frank communication restores the feeling of belonging after a reorganization. It's a feeling of "we weathered it through together," with emphasis on *we* and *together.*

Cell Manufacturing

Cell manufacturing is a first divergence from Henry Ford's conveyor line—a response to growing customer demand for variety and quality. It is ideal for labor-intensive assembly. A group of workers, each performing several tasks, build the product from start to finish, sometimes even including packaging and shipping. Advantages are better quality, greater flexibility, higher productivity, improved employee moral, and low in-process stocks.

Cell manufacturing eliminates the need for standby stocks as insurance against stopping a moving assembly line for lack of a component, or because of a defect detected too late. A single, slow cell-worker does not handicap an entire line. (Remember Charlie Chaplin in *Modern Times*?) A change in mix does not result in downtime. Each cell may produce a different product, or several different products. Workers can spot defects as they occur and can correct them immediately. Work is more challenging, jobs are less routine. Workers accompany their product to the finished stage, and thus identify with the result of their labor.

Not every product is suited for the cell process. For mass production of standard goods, moving assembly lines are still the solution.

Activity-based Accounting

In the fiscal area, activity-based costing (ABC) is a success for many. It paves the way to activity-based management, helping to run the business effectively. It's an answer to the eternal debate over indirect cost allocation. Rather than allocation to products or services by volume or time, it measures the real needs of the product/service. Those that require detailed planning, expensive processing, and more control are assigned those costs. Simple products become cheaper.

Work-flow Technique

Computer science and sophisticated software opened the door for work-flow technique. It breaks down departmental barriers and shows right away when something goes wrong. It replaces the class IPO (input-process-output) method and enables customized production. The principle is "computer conversation" among internal buyers and sellers. A request or offer is followed by negotiation, until buyer and seller reach an agreement. The assignment is then carried out and reported. The circle is closed by customer acceptance. The method is interesting for large and advanced organizations.

Multinational Trends

Another trend is in the organizational area. Global reorganization takes different organizational forms for worldwide exploitation of know-how and/or production and distribution of specific goods in the most effective way. Firms might use subcontracts, alliances, distribution networks, or licensing. A growing number of large firms aim for a direct presence worldwide. In manufacturing, availability of raw material, cheap or highly skilled labor, tax-breaks, and other considerations decide location. Such considerations may determine the source for worldwide supply of a specific part or product, in addition to serving the local market.

As with smaller firms, borderless multinational corporations need a common sense of purpose. Few have achieved it so far. Those that have are mostly highly specialized businesses with almost total product standardization worldwide. In these cases identical problems and similar solutions facilitate common language and operating procedures, resulting in a global culture.

Most other corporations, with major product diversification, have a more complicated problem. In the '60s, foreign affiliates of multinational corporations were generally managed by people from headquarters, who had little or no familiarity with the culture of the country in which they were working. Their gradual replacement by internationally experienced home, local, or third-country nationals was a move in the right direction. The trend is more and more toward locals in upper management of foreign subsidiaries. A remaining, occasional problem is communication between corporate headquarters staff who lack international know-how, and field operations.

During the '80s the matrix structure became popular, a restructuring along product lines. Multinational corporations maintained country headquarters with local management, and implemented simultaneous reporting to central product management. The reason behind this move was worldwide standardization of products, techniques, and procedures.

In some cases dual reporting created conflicts because of differences in interests and culture between local management and product-line management. As a consequence, several large organizations reverted to geographic organization, restricting dual reporting to finance.

With acquired experience every corporation looks for the organizational solution that best fits its particular needs. Now something new is emerging. Corporations now realize that to become a real multicultural multinational, they need more than just international expertise and local managers. Top management and board of directors must be multinational too. Globally reorganized top management is best prepared to understand, address, and eliminate cultural conflicts that arise between local customs and global policy. Such leadership can reconcile world-scale efficiency with national responsiveness and ensure global exchange of knowledge and new experiences.

Right decisions that meet both global and local requirements enhance common purpose.

EMERGING TRENDS

- *Integration beyond outsourcing.* The supplier assumes the entire design development. It's an emerging trend mainly in the automotive industry—a complete reversal of vertical integration. In this case, the industry restricts itself to basic design and assembly.

- *The virtual corporation.* Two or more companies have a close working relationship with no legal or ownership ties. The virtual corporation is a sum of assets and know-how. It has no employees of its own, no organization chart, nor legal address. By joining forces, each party contributes the best it has to offer to the common goal of increased sales and profits, without additional investment. A fit without a merger.

- *LBU, or leveraged build-ups (a modified version of LBO (leveraged buy-outs)).* The investor(s) pick and back a management team to make acquisitions in a given industry to build a focused company that can be floated at a later date.

- *Boardroom.* Trends in the boardroom are for increased accountability of the chief executive. Shareholders are gaining more say. Responsibility of outside directors is growing. The boss may get fired.

WHAT'S NEXT?

These are a few of the many trends. Some gain acceptance, others lose it. The principal move is toward the knowledge society. Knowledge will become the only meaningful resource. The change to knowledge as "the resource" makes society post-capitalist. "Management's task in the knowledge-based organization is to make everyone a contributor." [8]

FINAL CHECKLIST

- Use a method or system only if its fits your case.

- Introducing any new concept is difficult. You must commit to it and remain committed. In other words, never agree to something unless you know that you can do it and are determined to do it.

- Don't be satisfied with one option or recommendation. Ask for alternatives. Compare, measure, discuss, and decide.

The future is here. Where are you?

CONCLUSION

The *Checklist* does not say which roads to choose. There was no intention to do so. Decisions are yours to make. The *Checklist* may help in the process: inform, provoke, throw out ideas, help you think.

It's your privilege to disagree with the logic or arguments of the *Checklist*—but I hope it made you react and ponder, reaffirm or change your concepts. Use the *Checklist* as a refresher and a reference, as well as a checklist. Some readers may object to repetitions. But concepts, such as communication, creativity, or commitment, among others are integral parts of most management systems. To ignore a concept because it was mentioned before under another reference is to tell half the story.

A last reminder: *Business is service. The order goes to the one who serves the client best.*

And a last suggestion: Start applying *now* the ideas you found useful. Not tomorrow or next week, as we do with diets.

The near future remains full of challenges, demanding never-ending education. Fewer, if better, opportunities will require full-time production in half-time jobs. Management will have to be global and local at the same time; empower, yet stay in full control. Continuous changes and organizational flexibility will be planned, built-in features. Even mass production will survive only by incorporating customization—following customers' whims and fashions, and establishing niches. Only low-cost and high-quality products will find markets. As with their businesses, leaders too will enter global competition. Leaders will have to become global professionals, to use their knowledge and to exercise their professions anywhere.

But don't panic. Prepare.

NOTES

1. Mary Walton, *The Deming Management Method* (New York: G.P. Putnam's Sons, 1988).

2. William N. Yoeman, *1000 Things You Never Learned in Business School* (New York: Nal/Dutton, 1985).

3. Tom Peters, *Thriving on Chaos* (New York: Alfred A. Knopf, 1992).

4. John Updike, *The Witches of Eastwick* (New York: Alfred A. Knopf, 1984).

5. Dr. Meredith Belbin from the Industrial Training Research Unit at Cambridge (U.K.) led a seven-year test on teams at the Administration Staff College at Henley, Oxon (U.K.), as reported by Anthony Jay, author of *Corporate Man* and of *Management and Machiavelli.*

6. Michael Hammer and James Champy, *Reengineering the Corporation* (New York: Harper Collins, 1993)

7. Interview with Peter Drucker "Como enfrentar a Tempestade" (How to face the tempest), *EXAME,* May 1, 1991: 62/66.

8. Peter F. Drucker, *Post-Capitalist Society* (New York: Harper Business, 1993). Earlier, in *Management: Tasks, Responsibilities, Practices* (New York: Harper and Row, 1973), Peter Drucker wrote, "...increasingly the central human resources are not manual workers—skilled or unskilled—but knowledge workers." (p. 30). "Yesterday's middle management is being transformed into tomorrow's knowledge organization." (p. 450).

FURTHER READING

1. Dorine C. Andrews and Susan K. Stalick, *Business Reengineering—The Survival Guide* (New York: Prentice Hall, 1994).

2. Warren Bennis, *On Becoming a Leader* (Reading, Mass.: Addison-Wesley Publishing Company, 1989).

3. Brown, Hitchcock, and Willard, *Why TQM Fails and What to Do About It* (Burr Ridge, Ill.: Irwin Professional Publishing, 1994).

4. Michael Hammer and James Champy, *Reengineering the Corporation* (New York: Harper Collins Publishers, 1993).

5. Leonard R. Sayles, *The Working Leader* (New York: The Free Press, 1993).

6. Mary Walton, *Deming Management at Work* (New York: G.P. Putnam's Sons, 1990).

ABOUT THE AUTHOR

Gabriel Hevesi is Managing Partner of Target Ltd., a management consulting firm, based in Brazil. During 40 years of front-line business experience in three countries, he has been exposed to many different cultures and situations in different positions. His career ranges from running a small manufacturing operation (his own), to being architect, CEO, and country manager of a $200 million subsidiary of a large international corporation. He was elected Honorary Citizen of the State of Rio de Janeiro by the State Legislative Assembly in 1974. Mr. Hevesi studied economics in his native Hungary and graduated in textile engineering in Switzerland.

Gabriel Hevesi
Managing Partner
TARGET LTDA.
Av. Rio Branco 45 s/1305
20090 Rio de Janeiro, RJ
Brazil

PRAISE FOR THE MANAGEMENT MASTER SERIES

"A rare information resource.... Each book is a gem; each set of six books a basic library.... Handy guides for success in the '90s and the new millennium."

Otis Wolkins
Vice President Quality Services/Marketing
Administration, GTE

"Productivity Press has provided a real service in its *Management Master Series*. These little books fill the huge gap between the 'bites' of oversimplified information found in most business magazines and the full-length books that no one has enough time to read. They have chosen very important topics in quality and found well-known authors who are willing to hold themselves within the 'one plane trip's worth' length limitation. Every serious manager should have a few of these in their reading backlog to help keep up with today's new management challenges."

C. Jackson Grayson, Jr.
Chairman, American Productivity & Quality Center

"The *Management Master Series* takes the Cliffs Notes approach to management ideas, with each monograph a tight 50 pages of remarkably meaty concepts that are defined, dissected, and contextualized for easy digestion."

Industry Week

"A concise overview of the critical success factors for today's leaders."

Quality Digest

"A wonderful collection of practical advice for managers."

Edgar R. Fiedler
Vice President and Economic Counsellor,
The Conference Board

"A great resource tool for business, government, and education."

Dr. Dennis J. Murray
President, Marist College

PRODUCTIVITY PRESS, Dept. BK, PO Box 13390, Portland, OR 97213-0390
Telephone: 1-800-394-6868   Fax: 1-800-394-6286

THE MANAGEMENT MASTER SERIES

The Management Master Series offers business managers leading-edge information on the best contemporary management practices. Written by respected authorities, each short "briefcase book" addresses a specific topic in a concise, to-the-point presentation, using both text and illustrations. These are ideal books for busy managers who want to get the whole message quickly.

Great Management Ideas

Management Alert: Don't Reform—Transform!
Michael J. Kami
Transform your corporation: adapt faster, be more productive, perform better.

Vision, Mission, Total Quality: Leadership Tools for Turbulent Times
William F. Christopher
Build your vision and mission to achieve world class goals.

The Power of Strategic Partnering
Eberhard E. Scheuing
Take advantage of the strengths in your customer-supplier chain.

New Performance Measures
Brian H. Maskell
Measure service, quality, and flexibility with methods that address your customers' needs.

Motivating Superior Performance
Saul W. Gellerman
Use these key factors—non-monetary as well as monetary—to improve employee performance.

Doing and Rewarding: Inside a High-Performance Organization
Carl G. Thor
Design systems to reward superior performance and encourage productivity.

PRODUCTIVITY PRESS, Dept. BK, PO Box 13390, Portland, OR 97213-0390
Telephone: 1-800-394-6868   Fax: 1-800-394-6286

Total Quality

The 16-Point Strategy for Productivity and Total Quality
William F. Christopher/Carl G. Thor
Essential points you need to know to improve the performance of your organization.

The TQM Paradigm: Key Ideas That Make It Work
Derm Barrett
Get a firm grasp of the world-changing ideas beyond the Total Quality movement.

Process Management: A Systems Approach to Total Quality
Eugene H. Melan
Learn how a business process orientation will clarify and streamline your organization's capabilities.

Practical Benchmarking for Mutual Improvement
Carl G. Thor
Discover a down-to-earth approach to benchmarking and building useful partnerships for quality.

Mistake-Proofing: Designing Errors Out
Richard B. Chase and Douglas M. Stewart
Learn how to eliminate errors and defects at the source with inexpensive *poka-yoke* devices and staff creativity.

Communicating, Training, and Developing for Quality Performance
Saul W. Gellerman
Gain quick expertise in communication and employee development basics.

PRODUCTIVITY PRESS, Dept. BK, PO Box 13390, Portland, OR 97213-0390
Telephone: 1-800-394-6868   Fax: 1-800-394-6286

Customer Focus

Designing Products and Services That Customers Want
Robert King
Here are guidelines for designing customer-exciting products and services to meet the demands for continuous improvement and constant innovation to satisfy customers.

Creating Customers for Life
Eberhard E. Scheuing
Learn how to use quality function deployment to meet the demands for continuous improvement and constant innovation to satisfy customers.

Building Bridges to Customers
Gerald A. Michaelson
From the priceless value of a single customer to balancing priorities, Michaelson delivers a powerful guide for instituting a customer-based culture within any organization.

Delivering Customer Value: It's Everyone's Job
Karl Albrecht
This volume is dedicated to empowering people to deliver customer value and aligning a company's service systems.

Shared Expectations: Sustaining Customer Relationships
Wayne A. Little
How to create a process for sharing expectations and building lasting and profitable relationships with customers and suppliers that incorporates performance goals and measures.

Service Recovery: Fixing Broken Customers
Ron Zemke
Here are the guidelines for developing a customer-retaining service recovery system that can be a strategic asset in a company's total quality effort.

PRODUCTIVITY PRESS, Dept. BK, PO Box 13390, Portland, OR 97213-0390
Telephone: 1-800-394-6868   Fax: 1-800-394-6286

Leadership

Leading the Way to Organization Renewal
Burt Nanus
How to build and steer a continually renewing and transforming organization by applying a vision to action strategy.

Checklist for Leaders
Gabriel Hevesi
Learn to focus day-to-day decisions and actions, leadership, communications, team building, planning, and efficiency.

Creating Leaders for Tomorrow
Karl Albrecht
How to mobilize all the intelligence of the organization to create value for customers.

Total Quality: A Framework for Leadership
D. Otis Wolkins
Consider the problems and opportunities in today's world of changing technology, global competition, and rising customer expectations in terms of the leadership role.

From Management to Leadership
Lawrence M. Miller
A visionary analysis of the qualities required of leaders in today's business: vision and values, enthusiasm for customers, teamwork, and problem-solving skills at all levels.

High Performance Leadership: Creating Value in a World of Change
Leonard R. Sayles
Examine the need for leadership involvement in work systems and operations technology to meet the increasing demands for short development cycles and technologically complex products and services.

PRODUCTIVITY PRESS, Dept. BK, PO Box 13390, Portland, OR 97213-0390
Telephone: 1-800-394-6868   Fax: 1-800-394-6286

ABOUT PRODUCTIVITY PRESS

Productivity Press exists to support the continuous improvement of American business and industry.

Since 1983, Productivity has published more than 100 books on the world's best manufacturing methods and management strategies. Many Productivity Press titles are direct source materials translated for the first time into English from industrial leaders around the world.

The impact of the Productivity publishing program on Western industry has been profound. Leading companies in virtually every industry sector use Productivity Press books for education and training. These books ride the cutting edge of today's business trends and include books on total quality management (TQM), corporate management, Just-In-Time manufacturing process improvements, total employee involvement (TEI), profit management, product design and development, total productive maintenance (TPM), and system dynamics.

To get a copy of the full-color catalog, call 800-394-6868 or fax 800-394-6286.

To view sample chapters and see the complete line of books, visit the Productivity Press online catalog on the Internet at *http://www.ppress.com/*

Productivity Press titles are distributed to the trade by National Book Network, 800-462-6420

PRODUCTIVITY PRESS, Dept. BK, PO Box 13390, Portland, OR 97213-0390
Telephone: 1-800-394-6868   Fax: 1-800-394-6286

TO ORDER: Write, phone, or fax Productivity Press, Dept. BK, P.O. Box 13390, Portland, OR 97213-0390, phone 1-800-394-6868, fax 1-800-394-6286. Send check or charge to your credit card (American Express, Visa, MasterCard accepted).

U.S. ORDERS: Add $5 shipping for first book, $2 each additional for UPS surface delivery. Add $5 for each AV program containing 1 or 2 tapes; add $12 for each AV program containing 3 or more tapes. We offer attractive quantity discounts for bulk purchases of individual titles; call for more information.

ORDER BY E-MAIL: Order 24 hours a day from anywhere in the world. Use either address:
To order: *service@ppress.com*
To view the online catalog and/or order:
   http://www.ppress.com/

QUANTITY DISCOUNTS: For information on quantity discounts, please contact our sales department.

INTERNATIONAL ORDERS: Write, phone, or fax for quote and indicate shipping method desired. For international callers, telephone number is 503-235-0600 and fax number is 503-235-0909. Prepayment in U.S. dollars must accompany your order (checks must be drawn on U.S. banks). When quote is returned with payment, your order will be shipped promptly by the method requested.

NOTE: Prices are in U.S. dollars and are subject to change without notice.